David—
I thank God for you! You are an answer to prayer in my life! May God continue to bless your journey!

Jay

Feb 17, 2020

by jerry coleman

one-way ticket
leaving home for good

D1804501

© 2011 by Jerry Coleman

All rights reserved. No portion of this book may be reproduced, stored in a retrieval system, or transmitted in any form or by any means – electronic, mechanical, photocopy, recording, scanning, or other – except for brief quotations in critical reviews or articles, without the prior written permission of the publisher.

Published in Greenville, Illinois by Long Run Publications.

Cover design by Erin Newton
Book design by Erin Newton

Visit my website at *JerryColeman.org*

Scriptures taken from the Holy Bible, New International Version®, NIV®. Copyright © 1973, 1978, 1984 by Biblica, Inc.™ Used by permission of Zondervan. All rights reserved worldwide. www.zondervan.com

ISBN: 978-0-6154-6660-6

Printed in the United States of America

contents

Acknowledgments	5
Preface	6

leaving home   7

A Family That Prays Together, Scatters	9
Family Vote	13
Getting Started	19
Let's Go Sell Insurance	23
One Step	27

expanding home   29

New Leaders	31
Surprise in Galanta	35
Miriám-néni	37
A Night in the Orphan House	41
The Missing Flag	45
The Mester	49
A Missionary Life is a Lonely Life	52

harmonizing home   55

A Growing Chorus in Europe	57
Tears Flowed	61
It's a Long Way to Tipperary	63
Flight to Lisbon	65
You MUST Give More!	69
A Spontaneous Dance Broke Out	71
A Walk Around the Walls of Jerusalem	73

being home   77

Father's Day	79
My Home Base	83
Oh Pain, Pain	87
Miles and Miles	89
The Kids are Coming!	91
We Are Home	93

acknowledgments

I want to be quick to thank the many people who are part of my "home." I feel so rich knowing that I'm part of an extended family that lives in countless homes around the world!

I have known Doug Newton since the late 1980s. He brought tears to my eyes when he met with me on April 3, 2004 and shocked me with his perspective that, "You can write!" From then on, I took writing a bit more seriously and Doug has been a help and encouragement all along the way.

I first met Doug's daughter, Erin Newton, when she was a small girl. Her personal and professional development is evident in her design of this book and through many other publications. She has been a joy to work with! I feel as though she has brought the essence of these stories to visual life — helping our readers get into the heart of each one.

My daughter, Sarah, introduced me to a book and process called *The Artist's Way* by Julia Cameron. We decided to meet by phone for artistic encouragement on a regular basis. A lot of *One-Way Ticket* came out of this fun and challenging process with her.

Julie Allman came to me at a point when I was praying for someone to help as an "idea editor." She really helped me sort through ideas and was the first one to tell me, "I think you have a book here!"

The prayers and support of our parents and extended family have helped make our experiences blossom.

Our children, Sarah, Kristin and David, have lived most of these stories! One of my greatest joys in life is being their father!

My wife, Jan, has been a constant encourager and editor. She is my best friend and the one who readily travels with me on the *One-Way Ticket*.

preface

A One-Way Ticket took my family and me to Budapest, Hungary on August 13, 1996. Our three young children were immediately immersed into a local Hungarian elementary school. We tried to make a home in a foreign culture and in a language we couldn't speak.

Home in Europe meant a radical change in the kinds of things we saw, the kinds of people we met and our whole orientation on life. In the end, one by one, our children moved away from our European home and back to the USA. These are some stories from that clash of cultures, reflecting some of our surprises and some of our pain.

One-Way Ticket helps address the questions:
"What would it be like to live in another country?"
"What would it be like to take my family on a One-Way Ticket?"
"What would it be like to send a loved one far away from home?"
"What would it be like to *leave home for good*?"

For more information and interaction, go to: *JerryColeman.org*

leaving home

1996:
one last church
visit before
leaving home

a family that prays together, scatters

So THERE I SAT IN MY FAVORITE CHAIR...ON FATHER'S DAY...AND ALL ALONE. I KNEW I WOULD BE ALL ALONE ON THIS PARTICULAR DAY. I JUST HOPED THAT I WOULD HEAR FROM MY CHILDREN SCATTERED AROUND THE WORLD.

The *Tour de France* held my interest for awhile. I could closely follow one of the biggest sports events of the year – one of the benefits of living in Europe. Lance Armstrong returned to the race as the favorite...again.

But Father's Day is a family day! We honor fathers by bringing the family together for celebration. Where did it go wrong? Because on that day, we were all scattered on three different continents, four countries and all different area codes. All three grown children had taken off! They had left home. They landed somewhere else far, far away.

"Hello!" I picked up the phone with hope!

"Happy Father's Day, Dad!" Ah, all fell back into place. It's like she's right next door! Yes, we had been a close family. We planted and led churches first in mid-west America, then in central Europe. Our whole family of five (now six) became involved in living for Jesus and inviting others to do the same.

Times around the dinner table and before bed became opportunities for prayer. We reviewed the day, celebrated the victories, encouraged each other through difficulties and prayed for more of God's blessings. I could always depend on the circle of family.

Until now. When I sat thousands of miles away. Following Armstrong's yellow jersey didn't fill the gap. My comfortable chair wasn't enough. Oh, to reverse the clock and get back to the "good old days!"

"Hello," I answered again.

"Happy Father's Day!" another celebrated.

It slowly began to sink in… that these three (and four by marriage) were really happy! They loved where they were! Ready to leave, to live on their own, they chose these unique places and responsibilities. I began to see a powerful unity of family and separation.

We would sometimes travel together to another city or country to sing, dramatize and tell our God-stories. We voted as a family to actually move out of a comfortable suburban setting in America to land in an unknown world and environment. We did this together. For a common purpose. But a few years ago, each one began to "fly out of the nest" and into a world of their own. Each one has the power to create family and have a vote of their own.

"Hello," hoping this would be the third.

"Happy Father's Day!" now celebrating with the one farthest away.

It's true that as the followers of Jesus grew closer to Him and His heart, they were willing to move away from Him. The more love and grace they experienced, the more they had to give away. The more of the Kingdom of God they saw, the more they wanted to show the Kingdom to others.

---

isaiah 6:3,8

"HOLY, HOLY, HOLY IS THE LORD ALMIGHTY; THE WHOLE EARTH IS FULL OF HIS GLORY."

THEN I HEARD THE VOICE OF THE LORD SAYING, "WHOM SHALL I SEND? AND WHO WILL GO FOR US?"

AND I SAID, "HERE AM I. SEND ME!"

So, they traveled to the ends of the earth, sacrificing family ties, comforts and reputations.

So, I had always heard that, "The family that prays together, stays together." I don't think this can sum up the whole truth. Sure, our family prayed together…every day. Now, well, the distance could hardly be greater between us!

But the more I thought about it, the more I wouldn't want it any other way. Proximity is one thing, but sharing a common heart for our Heavenly Father brings such unity that I could celebrate distance! One lonely hour after the other, I sat in Budapest, Hungary with a heart of celebration! I rejoiced with the two in Indonesia. I rejoiced with the one in St Louis. I rejoiced with the other in Los Angeles. I rejoiced with my wife in Slovakia helping to care for a new born. Day by day, step by step – I began to see something more powerful than "staying together."

Even the Father in heaven was willing to send His one and only Son far, far away. They shared a common purpose. And were willing to make great personal sacrifices for the good of others, for the good of the whole.

I bless my daughter. I bless my son-in-law. I bless my daughter. I bless my son. They live and breathe and travel and move to the sounds and voices of One beyond me. Each one heard the voice to go and to speak and to show up in far away geographical places.

With the last of my "Father's Day" phone conversations at an end, I sat there with a couple of tears running down my face. This was a good day! Yes, I did feel the pain of distance. But I felt the closeness of each one. Following a couple of decades of prayer, a unique purpose unfolded for each member of the family. One day at a time, one risk at a time has put great distance between us. What a celebration!

A family that prays together, scatters.

Coleman family prayer card (1990)

family vote

That moment would determine the rest of our lives. The family vote was set for Saturday at two in the afternoon. The final decision to move our family halfway around the world to a totally new country, language and lifestyle now lay at the influence of our children – ages seven, eight and eleven. The meeting was called to order around the dining room table. What would they decide?

"OK, now, the question is this – 'Do we move to Hungary?' Everyone will have two votes. The most votes win." This introduced the meeting.

"Wow. This really sounds democratic," I thought to myself. A family should be run autocratically or at least patristically (from a father's perspective). But for some reason my wife, Jan, and I decided it best to put it to a Family Vote.

"First of all, let's make a chart of our lives." Using five different colors of markers – which, of course, Kristin supplied – we began plotting our lives out on the time line.

"1958 – Dad is born in Columbus, Ohio.
"1958 – Mom is born in Chicago Heights, Illinois."

These were two separate dots on the chart – two people born far away from each other and at the beginning of time. The next dot on the time line was one dot for two people meeting at Greenville College in 1976. Yes, they all knew the story by heart of our meeting each other during Freshman Orientation.

"1978 – Mom and Dad are married and move to Columbus, Ohio. Mom to finish college and Dad to work with Papa.
"1982 – Mom and Dad are called to ministry and move back to Greenville for more schooling.
"1984 – A new color is added! Sarah Elizabeth is born in Greenville, Illinois!
"1984 – We move to Wilmore, Kentucky to attend seminary.
"1986 – We move to Wenatchee, Washington for a one year pastoral internship.
"1987 – A new color is added! Kristin Ruth is born in Wenatchee, Washington!"

By that time, the chart was nearly covered with dots and lines and colors. The children knew all these stories and all these places and all these colors. But we had never seen it all drawn out before.

"1987 – We move to Nicholasville, Kentucky to finish seminary and to pastor a local church.
"1988 – A new color is added! Jonathan David is born in Lexington, Kentucky!
"1990 – Dad finally graduates from seminary and we move to Indianapolis, Indiana for Dad to work with Free Methodist World Missions.
"1992 – We move to St. Louis, Missouri for Dad to pastor the West County Fellowship."

The kids asked a few questions along the way. As a result of seeking God's leading through the years, this chart exploded with color and movement. The dots and lines highlighted our life stories. But only one question remained. I felt nervous waiting for the answer.

A couple of weeks before the Family Vote, Jan and I had spent a week in Hungary on a discernment trip. Over the course of that week we sometimes felt the excitement of fitting into the familiar ministry of church planting and teaching English as a foreign language. Let's go!

But in contrast, we could feel the weight of trying to adapt to a new and foreign culture with the most difficult language in Europe – Hungarian. We would plan to immerse those precious three into Hungarian schools.

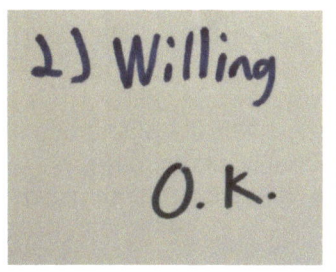

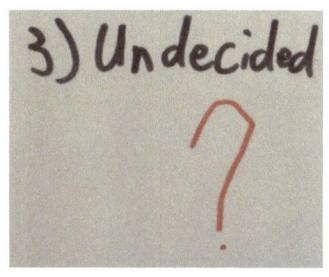

Vote cards

We visited an elementary school in Győr, a city in western Hungary where we were invited to serve. Walking out of the school, Jan and I glanced at each other with the same thought, "I don't think we can do this." But the will of God and the will of the family? This I wanted to know – I thought.

"Now, it's 1996," I continued. "Here we are in St. Louis. Do we move to Hungary or stay in St. Louis?" Silence. The timeline ended. This is it.

I distributed the five sets of four 3" x 5" cards that Kristin helped me create. These would represent our vote. One card had "Yes" written on it. The next said "Willing." The third card had a big question mark on it, meaning "I am undecided." And the fourth card had "No" on it, voting to stay in St. Louis.

I tried to keep my voice steady, saying, "OK, now the rules are that in just a moment, we will all hold the cards under the table and pick two. After that, each one of us will place those two cards on the table, one at a time, going from youngest to oldest.

"Oh, there's one more rule. Each one of us can ask one question about your vote."

"Well, are we ready?" Was I ready to see the evidence of what was going on in the minds of our young children? Jan and I had been home from Hungary for a week. We had explained what we saw and learned there. We told the good and the bad. We asked all three to be praying and thinking before we voted as a family.

"One more thing. Let's pray first." I voiced a last desperate prayer. Please guide us, O Lord, and so on. I couldn't put it off any longer.

Everyone kind of smiled as we all secretly voted with quick peeks at the shuffling of cards under the table. David's head barely reached above the table. Kristin was smiling. Was it because we had used HER dry erase board and HER markers and HER drawn out cards? Sarah looked a bit more serious as she most times did. Life in Sarah's brain had already taken the turn toward adulthood. Jan and I just nervously looked at each other and at our young offspring.

"OK, David, you're first. Your two cards, please."

He suddenly did what I had never calculated. Jan and I had discussed the idea of picking only ONE card. I thought two might be more expressive of what was really going on inside. But I never imagined that these two cards would show up at the same time.

"Yes." And "No."

I kept my quick reaction to myself, "WHAT!? Why did you pick two opposing cards!? You can't do that!"

"OK, now it's time to ask one question. Kristin, you are first."

"David," Kristin asked, "Why did you pick 'No'?"

"Well, I don't wanna leave my friends, like Andrew and Mark. And I don't wanna leave my school."

It's true. We lived in a very desirable area of St. Louis. The children attended schools in the Rockwood school district, which was rated one of the top in Missouri. Each of the kids had a room of their own in our four-bedroom home. We all enjoyed the suburban American life with two cars parked in an attached two-car garage with an automatic garage door opener. Yet, there was something more. We weren't so rich. But we had so much more than a large portion of the world. Libraries, books, training, experience, resources, family, faith and loving support – just to name a few. Maybe it was time to share – even at great expense.

We all understood David's first answer. Sarah asked him a question about making new friends. Then, Jan simply asked, "Why did you pick 'Yes'?"

Our seven year old youngest spoke up with a little smile on his face, "I'll go if you buy me a Nintendo game system."

Everyone chuckled after hearing his answer. The pressure in the room eased a bit. Oh, that's it!? He would get on an airplane with a one-way ticket in exchange for a video game!? I wondered what else we would hear today.

Kristin. Then Sarah. Jan. Then me. By the end, ten cards circled the table with five "Yes," four "Willing," and one "No" answers.

"Well, all of us said 'Yes.' We have all answered 'Yes' to this possible move to Hungary. So, I would like us to stand, hold hands around this table and pray, declaring our answer to the Lord."

We prayed. It was done. We would go. That was our final answer.

Two weeks after this vote, Jan and I sat in our final interview. We were approved.

Two months after this vote, we started visiting churches for prayer and financial support. We were soon fully funded.

Five months after this vote, we flew with one-way tickets through Detroit, Amsterdam and finally landing in Budapest.

The rest of our lives *were* changed. By that Family Vote.

```
MTS TRAVEL                      CLIENT: COLEMAN/JERRY
123 EAST MAIN ST HEINTZ BLDG STE 204
MONROE            WA      360 805-0864    INVOICE: 607106812  PAGE:01
----------------------------------------------------------------------
 13 AUG    KLM              FLIGHT: 5180    CLASS:  H
   TU      INDIANAPOLIS     DEPART: 1050A    VIA: NORTHWEST AIRLINES
           DETROIT/METRO    ARRIVE:  102P

 13 AUG    KLM              FLIGHT: 8068    CLASS:  H
   TU      DETROIT/METRO    DEPART:  530P    VIA: NORTHWEST AIRLINES
           AMSTERDAM        ARRIVE:  710A 14AUG

 14 AUG    KLM              FLIGHT:  253    CLASS:  H
   WE      AMSTERDAM        DEPART:  850A
           BUDAPEST         ARRIVE: 1055A

                                             TICKET: 0741465737147
                                             FARE:         USD853.00
```

```
MTS TRAVEL                      CLIENT: COLEMAN/JANICE
123 EAST MAIN ST HEINTZ BLDG STE 204
MONROE            WA      360 805-0864    INVOICE: 607106812  PAGE:01
----------------------------------------------------------------------
 13 AUG    KLM              FLIGHT: 5180    CLASS:  H
   TU      INDIANAPOLIS     DEPART: 1050A    VIA: NORTHWEST AIRLINES
           DETROIT/METRO    ARRIVE:  102P

 13 AUG    KLM              FLIGHT: 8068    CLASS:  H
   TU      DETROIT/METRO    DEPART:  530P    VIA: NORTHWEST AIRLINES
           AMSTERDAM        ARRIVE:  710A 14AUG

 14 AUG    KLM              FLIGHT:  253    CLASS:  H
   WE      AMSTERDAM        DEPART:  850A
           BUDAPEST         ARRIVE: 1055A

                                             TICKET: 0741465737148
                                             FARE:         USD853.00
```

```
MTS TRAVEL                      CLIENT: COLEMAN/SARAH
123 EAST MAIN ST HEINTZ BLDG STE 204
MONROE            WA      360 805-0864    INVOICE: 607106812  PAGE:01
----------------------------------------------------------------------
 13 AUG    KLM              FLIGHT: 5180    CLASS:  H
   TU      INDIANAPOLIS     DEPART: 1050A    VIA: NORTHWEST AIRLINES
           DETROIT/METRO    ARRIVE:  102P

 13 AUG    KLM              FLIGHT: 8068    CLASS:  H
   TU      DETROIT/METRO    DEPART:  530P    VIA: NORTHWEST AIRLINES
           AMSTERDAM        ARRIVE:  710A 14AUG

 14 AUG    KLM              FLIGHT:  253    CLASS:  H
   WE      AMSTERDAM        DEPART:  850A
           BUDAPEST         ARRIVE: 1055A

                                             TICKET: 0741465737149
                                             FARE:         USD853.00
```

```
MTS TRAVEL                      CLIENT: COLEMAN/KIRSTIN MISS
123 EAST MAIN ST HEINTZ BLDG STE 204
MONROE            WA      360 805-0864    INVOICE: 607106813  PAGE:01
----------------------------------------------------------------------
 13 AUG    KLM              FLIGHT: 5180    CLASS:  H
   TU      INDIANAPOLIS     DEPART: 1050A    VIA: NORTHWEST AIRLINES
           DETROIT/METRO    ARRIVE:  102P

 13 AUG    KLM              FLIGHT: 8068    CLASS:  H
   TU      DETROIT/METRO    DEPART:  530P    VIA: NORTHWEST AIRLINES
           AMSTERDAM        ARRIVE:  710A 14AUG

 14 AUG    KLM              FLIGHT:  253    CLASS:  H
   WE      AMSTERDAM        DEPART:  850A
           BUDAPEST         ARRIVE: 1055A

                                             TICKET: 0741465737150
                                             FARE:         USD649.00
```

```
MTS TRAVEL                      CLIENT: COLEMAN/DAVID MSTR
123 EAST MAIN ST HEINTZ BLDG STE 204
MONROE            WA      360 805-0864    INVOICE: 607106813  PAGE:01
----------------------------------------------------------------------
 13 AUG    KLM              FLIGHT: 5180    CLASS:  H
   TU      INDIANAPOLIS     DEPART: 1050A    VIA: NORTHWEST AIRLINES
           DETROIT/METRO    ARRIVE:  102P

 13 AUG    KLM              FLIGHT: 8068    CLASS:  H
   TU      DETROIT/METRO    DEPART:  530P    VIA: NORTHWEST AIRLINES
           AMSTERDAM        ARRIVE:  710A 14AUG

 14 AUG    KLM              FLIGHT:  253    CLASS:  H
   WE      AMSTERDAM        DEPART:  850A
           BUDAPEST         ARRIVE: 1055A

                                             TICKET: 0741465737151
                                             FARE:         USD649.00
```

The Coleman family's one-way tickets from the U.S. to Budapest

| *getting started* |

WHEN WE GOT OFF THE PLANE, THREE CO-WORKERS MET US AND CRAMMED OUR 20 BAGS, FIVE CARRY-ONS, ALONG WITH A DOG AND HIS KENNEL INTO A VAN. THE HOUR AND A HALF ROAD TRIP SEEMED LIKE NOTHING COMPARED TO THE THREE ONE-WAY FLIGHTS, LEAVING OUR FAMILY AND FRIENDS BEHIND. CARRYING EVERYTHING UP THOSE THREE FLIGHTS OF STAIRS SEEMED LIKE A WALK IN THE PARK COMPARED TO SELLING OUR HOME IN ST. LOUIS AND SORTING EVERYTHING WE OWNED INTO THREE PILES: 1) TAKE, 2) GIVE AWAY, 3) STORE IN MOM AND DAD'S BARN.

They showed us our new home – a half furnished, small three bedroom apartment on the third floor – while our dog, Shadow, joyfully found the cool place under the dining room table much better than the belly of three airplanes.

Our son, David, fell asleep sitting up on the couch. Our daughter, Kristin, soon began playing with three Hungarian girls in the courtyard. Our daughter, Sarah, helped unpack. After co-workers helped us carry everything up, they called for pizza and left us with a prayer and a blessing to learn the language and plant churches. Then they were gone. Back to their own homes…an hour and a half away.

We were there. Just us. Alone. With a dog. Heads spinning. Quiet house. Sounds of motor-scooters passing on the street. Sounds of cars with two cycle engines. Smells of concrete and old world. Interior colors new to us. Emergency sirens with strange patterns. Swollen ankles. Tired bones. Weak knees. Little faith.

During seminary, I bought into the principle of being immersed into the language and culture. I got great grades in seminary. But now the real test began! We could count to ten in Hungarian (note: I could only count to three). What would we do for dinner? Could we actually throw our three young treasures into Hungarian school!?

School started the first of September in a way I had never dreamed. Dressed in the traditional black and white celebration uniform, the whole student body stood in the enclosed concrete courtyard and we heard the sounds of a new Hungarian school year for the very first time. Flutes, student choir, national anthem, folk dance, long speech.

I'm sure this felt normal to some people. This atmosphere was totally beyond my imagination. The air stood still as sweat ran down my back. The constant chatting of parents around me during the ceremony raised so many questions in my mind that I couldn't begin to articulate even one.

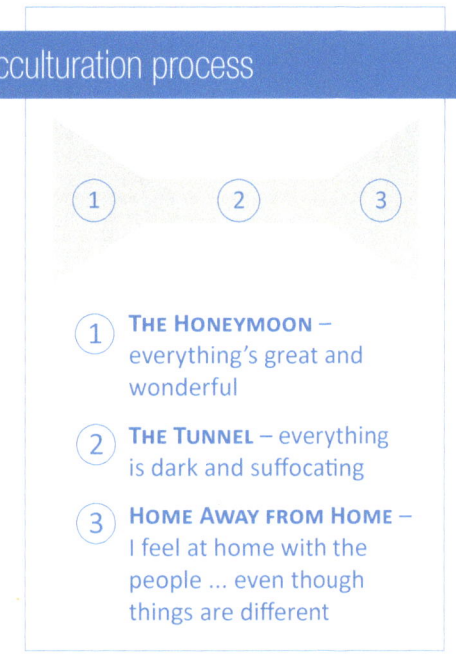

acculturation process

1. **The Honeymoon** – everything's great and wonderful
2. **The Tunnel** – everything is dark and suffocating
3. **Home Away from Home** – I feel at home with the people ... even though things are different

Every subsequent evening provided complex detective work. For example, the translated note from the English teacher read, "Your children must bring the elevenses every day." What does this possibly mean? And this was in English! Yes, our children MUST bring it! Every day! But what? The ELEVENSES! What are the elevenses?

The English-Hungarian dictionary describes, "Elevenses: tízórai" (literally, "Elevenses: ten o'clocks"). Jan calls out to the children, "What happens at ten o'clock on a daily basis?!"

"We have snacks! Everyone brings a snack to eat mid morning," Kristin answered.

Next note from David's teacher and translated by the English teacher, "Please send a towel with David to put under the elevenses!" There was stronger language to this letter as his teacher was rather exasperated with us. Every good parent knows that a towel is needed with the elevenses!

Homework. This made the elevenses issue look easy. "A 'k'- val kezdődő szavakat húzd alá!" Literal translation: "The 'k' - with starts words underline below."

Well, was that a puppy or a dog? An apple or a peach? This one exercise took an hour and a half with books, dictionaries and finally a run to the neighbor who spoke some English. It took our neighbor 30 seconds.

I threw what I learned in seminary out the window. My experience from business and pastoring two churches meant little here. I merely focused on communicating on a pre-two-year-old level: "Me want one. Yes, those one. What money? Have. Bye-bye."

We call this period "The Tunnel." (It follows "The Honeymoon" when everything seems new and exciting. That was long gone.) It seemed like we'd never get out of "The Tunnel," make sense of it all and enjoy life once again.

Forced back to the basics with pat answers eluding me, I had little choice but to turn directly to Jesus. My good-solid-suburban American way failed me here. I prayed and prayed and prayed for God to show me a way of survival: God, Bible, prayer, people. That's all I had. Is that all I needed?

The quickest way out of a tunnel is to back out. Right back from where we came! This tempted me. For me, this sounded refreshing most nights.

But in the morning was Jesus. He waited for me. He met me morning by morning. He led my family all the way here to these people. He would not abandon us. If I am in "The Tunnel," I am in it with Him...and He with me.

Coleman family prayer card (1996)

let's go sell insurance

hen Jan and I hit that third step, climbing the stairs once again to our Hungarian language class, we just turned to each other.

"Let's go sell insurance."

Serving as a pastoral couple in the USA had been quite challenging at times. We had this private joke between us when the people would begin to get on our nerves. "Let's go sell insurance." I had been a productive businessman in the past. I had been offered jobs that would have made us quite comfortable in suburban life. But we found ourselves in the middle of Europe trying to learn the most difficult European language while immersing our three children into the local Hungarian school. Our ministry goal was to plant a church in the midst of a people we could not even begin to understand.

All we could see before us was a huge mountain that flight of stairs represented.

We had tried to live by a certain rule in ministry: If one spouse is struggling, the other had to be positive and encouraging. Thankfully, this usually worked! But our rule absolutely broke down on that day in December – just four months after arriving. On the third step.

I began forming in my mind what I would announce around the dinner table that night. "OK, kids, I have some good news! You don't have to go back to that school again. You don't have to struggle any more. You don't have to try to make new friends here. Tomorrow, we are all going to start packing and head back home. I'm going to get a new job and we can go back to living the way we used to."

We no longer would have to struggle just to find out the very basic needs of life – like, light bulbs. I remember one day around the dinner table answering our daily question, "What's one good thing that happened to you today?"

"I found a light bulb!!!" I felt so proud of myself after heading out the door and four hours later coming back with a replacement bulb. I went to the first store on Baross Street, walked in and held up the bulb. "Me. Want. One."

They told me, "Itt nem kapható! A másik boltba kell menni!"

I gave a blank stare, "What?"

Then, the lady started drawing a little map and pointing out the door while saying stuff that left me looking blank. With the map in hand and the burned-out bulb in the other, I left. Getting nowhere, I showed the map to some stranger on the street.

"Ott lesz! Csak oda kell menni! Közel van!" he said, pointing further down the street.

So, this went on for some time and finally after wandering around town and finding the fifth store, I had the replacement bulb in my hands and started home like an exhausted hunter.

But we came to plant a church. Before arriving with our 20 bags, five carry-ons and one dog, we knew exactly one person within the 100 kilometer radius. But we had not yet met this gal personally. And she had just moved to this city one week before we arrived. She had met one person – the secretary of the Hungarian language school. And this was our base for planting a church? Two people?

"Let's go sell insurance."

After making our way up the fourth, fifth and then three dozen steps,

I vaguely remember sitting through the four hours of language class. (It actually only ends up being three hours because Hungarians figure a professional hour is 45 minutes with a 15 minute break!? This was ANOTHER thing that really bothered me!) My dreadful delight to begin packing up as soon as possible occupied my mind through the morning.

But on the walk home from language class, Jan said, "You know, we're not finished here yet…."

"What? What do you mean not finished?"

"Well, I don't know much at all today," she continued. "But I *do* know that God called us and led us here. For some reason. That much was clear to us earlier this year."

I had to agree with her on that. We heard God's voice. We saw Him open up so many doors and ways and paths. The five of us had celebrated the beginning of a new stage in life. And our family, our friends, our churches blessed and supported us all along the way.

"So, what are you saying?" I asked, not wanting to hear the answer.

"Well, I think we need to wait another day before we tell the kids to start packing up."

Time stopped, stood still as we continued walking past the bus station, the train station, the city hall, the bread store, the watch store. A new neighbor waved "Halló" interrupting my inner thunderstorm. I just wanted to pack up and leave.

Around the dinner table that night, I don't remember my answer to "What's one good thing that happened to you today?" Maybe it was something about what I had for lunch that day. But I did *not* announce that we were packing up.

One more night. One more day. One more step.

We soon put up our Christmas tree. Neighbors gave us very curious looks. We asked our language teacher about this. She said that only on

December 24 do "Little Jesus and the angels" bring the Christmas tree. "So, for us, it's very strange to see a tree up and decorated two weeks before Christmas," she chuckled. We went on to celebrate that first Christmas without our extended family.

By January, things began to look a little brighter. It could have been the constant falling of fresh, clean snow. Our children's school held their annual family ski camp. We signed up. Our days brightened! Ski. Eat. Play games. Sleep. I could handle this life. At least for a week.

We decided to host an English Camp for youth the following summer. This project brought focus – to communicate the love of Jesus in our community through a felt need – the need to learn English.

Jan coordinated the English instruction. I focused on logistics, games and overall leadership. Our children invited their friends. A ministry team came from Kansas. Registrations filled our 60 slots! Over five days, we played games, sang Christian music, gave personal testimonies of God's life changing power and had all kinds of fun together!

By the end, several young people prayed to enter into a relationship with Jesus to begin a new life. Wow! This is it!

One year after landing, my eyes began to see The Divine Plan unfolding. These few days began to give meaning to why we were here. We saw new light at the end of the long darkness.

We went on to plant that first church that began in our living room. Our children went on to finish Hungarian 6th, 8th and 12th grades, respectively. Only recently did we share with them about that third step going up to language class and how close we came to packing it up. We all learned though, to take…one step at a time.

one step

What is it that will bring us together?
What is it that cuts us apart?

Who is willing to lay down one's life
To save the whole?

Where is the forgiveness without the pain?
Where is the new without the old?

How will it be when I can't picture the now?
How will it flow when nothing is going?

Why did this happen
When all was so perfect and whole?

Why did the shortcuts
Cut us all short?

So, now
Now is the moment to choose
The moment to go forward
Even in pain and clouds.

The step, the one
Which will begin
Be a start
Just one
Now.

expanding home

Coleman family prayer card (1998)

| new leaders |

I DECIDED TO PUT THIS BIBLICAL STUFF TO THE TEST. WE NEEDED LEADERS. HUNGARIAN LEADERS.

At the summer English Camp in 1997 quite a few youth in the community became curious about Jesus. So, we invited a dozen of these youth who showed leadership potential to our flat. Some of them were confessed believers in Jesus, some of them weren't, others just weren't sure. But all of them shared the excitement of finding something new and different at camp.

That Saturday, after piling all their shoes just inside our front door, and after kissing everyone on both cheeks, and after filling them up on chips, biscuits and drinks, and after singing some familiar camp songs, and after shouting stories across our living room about the joys of camp, we asked them if they thought others in Győr would like this kind of thing to happen on a regular basis.

"Some of you have experienced something significant – a personal contact with Jesus. Would you be interested in telling your friends about this and helping them to have personal contact with Jesus too?"

They all were enthusiastic and ready to go! "Persze! Of course!"

I grew up in the USA. I was formally trained in the USA. I was part of the American church for many years. The primary model I saw was that of THE pastor, THE minister, personally performing THE ministry. This was how it all got done!

While living in Hungary and searching for new answers, I began to scratch my head a bit. I struggled to find the biblical model of just one person doing all the church stuff.

In the book of Acts I read about the spontaneous expansion of the church with "unschooled, ordinary men (and women)." John Wesley talked about the "Priesthood of all believers," but had I really seen this in action? I tried to believe that God, Himself, could raise up new leaders – right here, right now.

So, we encouraged the teens to brainstorm about ideas on what to do next. They came up with the idea of having a one day camp reunion when they would also invite other friends to join in the experience.

"That's a great idea!" I affirmed. "Now, let's get into four planning groups. We need a publicity group, a music and drama group, a game group and an overall leadership group that would help keep us all on track."

So, we immediately got into the groups: one stayed in the living room, one went to the girls' bedroom, one sat on the floor of the master bedroom and one sat around the dining table.

"OK, the first thing you need to do is pick a leader and an assistant leader. Then start planning."

At first they were rather shocked and surprised that we wanted them to actually initiate and lead. My wife, another adult and I simply encouraged them and answered questions. By the end of the evening, there was so much energy in our flat that we didn't need light bulbs!

Two months later, I stood in the back of the rented hall and watched these teens lead music, dramatize a story, lead games and share personal stories about how Jesus was making a difference in their lives. The Spirit of God was raising up a new generation. Faith was springing up into reality.

So, we're trying something different. We're trying something biblical. Those teens who crowded into our apartment are now scattered throughout Hungary and across Europe. Some of them have become very strong Christian leaders. Some have drifted away. But we all experienced the power of God's reality that each one of us can be a leader for change.

Coleman family prayer card (2002)

surprise in galanta

T HE PUNKS STARTED TO SHOW UP. WE DIDN'T REALLY EXPECT THIS. WE PREPARED OURSELVES TO MEET SOME NICE YOUNG PEOPLE WHO WOULD ENJOY A CHRISTIAN CONCERT. INSTEAD, WE LOOKED OUT TO A HANDFUL DRESSED IN BLACK WITH BODY PIERCINGS AND CHAINS.

"Let's pray!" I announced, bringing the team back behind the curtain. The ten youth gathered in a circle, nervously glanced at one another, and then we all turned to the One above and beyond.

"OK, bring it on!" I encouraged as I went to sit down. "Az Élet Fénye" was the name for the group of teenagers from Győr who joined together to sing, act, share testimonies and try to bring the message of Jesus to people who had not yet heard. This brought us to Galanta, Slovakia through a contact from one of the youth. It was advertised in town as a free concert. But we never imagined THIS crowd!

Sarah led the band in the first set. The crowd of a dozen people pretty much talked amongst themselves while a few more straggled in.

Kristin led in a drama – showing without words the crucifixion and resurrection of Jesus. This seemed to catch the imagination of this group with the short attention span of young children.

We tried to get the audience back into the building after their smoke break. The leaders up front encouraged the crowd to shake tambourines, clap their hands and basically join the band. The main punk leader jumped on stage, at the encouragement of all his buddies, and sat down to beat a drum center stage.

Some danced, some sat, but we noticed that all started connecting. The testimony came from Dalma. Everyone listened intently. Something new. Something very strange. This is about Jesus? Here from this city stage?

We could see some of the façade give way to a genuine interest in something that would give meaning to an empty life. Questions were being asked. Yes, there is more. There is more to life than darkness. Yes, there is hope. Yes, there is the possibility to go personal – straight to Jesus and Jesus to you.

We concluded with everyone standing, some dancing in the aisles. But this unusual crowd quickly went away after thanking us for coming. Would we ever see them again?

The packing and drive home took on a different buzz. Surprise, joy and faith sprung alive with chatter and smiles and laughter. Who would have guessed? We expected a "nice" crowd. Instead, a wild group of punks heard the life changing message of Jesus – perhaps for the very first time.

Miriám-néni

I HESITANTLY WALKED UP THE STEPS TO THE MUSIC SCHOOL. I HAD BEEN THERE DOZENS OF TIMES, BUT NEVER IN ANTICIPATION OF A SENSITIVE MEETING LIKE THIS. MY DAUGHTER'S MUSIC THEORY TEACHER, THE SWEET MIRIÁM-NÉNI, WOULD OPEN MY WORLD TO A SHOCKING REALITY CLOSE TO HOME.

The Holocaust seemed so long ago and far away. Yes, I had been towed through the Holocaust museum in Jerusalem and nearly gagged at seeing the mounds of hair, hair combs and buttons at Auschwitz. But the conversation with my daughter's teacher, an offspring of two Auschwitz survivors, made the Holocaust a living reality.

Castles Burning, a memoir by Magda Denes, opened my eyes to brutal realities that happened close to my new home in Central Europe. Denes described her pre-teen descent from playing piano in her elegant home on the Danube River, to surviving years of life on the run in a world of shame. Initiating a visit with Miriám-néni had little to do with an interest in history or war or East versus West. It had to do with my great sorrow over the stories lying quietly under the surface all around me.

I had to know more, hear more. Determinedly, I made that appointment with Miriám-néni. Hesitantly, I stepped up those stairs while hearing the traditional music flowing from all the practice rooms.

"Have a seat, Jerry."

"Thank you. I've been reading this book. And, well..." I tried to continue. "Well, the history that I learned as a kid isn't so far away from me now, is it?"

Since moving to Hungary, I had purchased a map showing the sites where Jews were rounded up, forced into train cars and taken away. One site was right next door to where my son attended school. Shortly into our conversation, I learned that Miriám-néni's whole family left from that very spot.

"The officers announced that in thirty minutes they had to be ready to leave with one small bag each. My grandparents hurriedly packed what they could, but felt certain they would be back after this short disruption."

Long ago my mind had absorbed school lesson details about this period of time. My heart had been opened as I read *Castles Burning*. But in those moments I began to feel overwhelmed by this personal story of someone so close to our family.

"My parents were forced to wear the yellow star. All Jews were! But then, that one day, all had to leave, not knowing where they would be led and not knowing when they would be back. My parents' families lived near each other and attended that big synagogue there on Zsidó Square. You know, the one that's now a 'culture center'."

"How could it become a culture center?"

"That used to be the biggest synagogue in Western Hungary.

trust me!

OUR NEIGHBORS HAVE HEARD IT ALL THROUGH HISTORY:

HAPSBURG SAID, "TRUST ME! I WILL DELIVER YOU FROM THE SOUTH!"

STALIN SAID, "TRUST ME! I WILL DELIVER YOU FROM THE WEST!"

HITLER SAID, "TRUST ME! I WILL DELIVER YOU FROM THE EAST!"

WE SAY, "TRUST ME! JESUS WILL DELIVER YOU!"

OUR NEIGHBORS SAY, "YEAH, RIGHT....I'VE HEARD THAT BEFORE."

Beautiful! Gorgeous! You can see the pictures in this book. But it was badly damaged during the war and was never fixed up until two years ago. Now, the city has taken it over as a culture center."

"But wasn't that the property of the local Jewish community?"

"Sure it was!" she laughed at my narrow, western mind-set of ownership and property. "They just took it! It's theirs. We could do nothing about it!"

"Oh."

"My parents were very young. And they were the only two from both families to survive Auschwitz. They somehow returned and were soon married. That's when I came along." She smiled and subtly noted the miraculous gift of her one life among slaughter.

The faint tones I could still hear in the music school just sounded distorted to me. "Do people here at the music school know this story? Do they realize what happened?"

"Oh, some do, but most – especially the kids – will make some *really* rude comments – and I'm standing right there! You wouldn't believe these comments. But I'm used to it. I can't do anything about it."

I wished I could. I was ready to stand guard around her and fight off any and all who said or did anything cruel. I wanted to turn back the clocks and stop all the killing and destruction, and the selection of what person is worthy and which person is not. Are not all created in the image of God?

"The worst of it all was when my father returned. He managed to find his parents' flat. It was still there. But absolutely empty. Empty! The neighbors, the same neighbors who he had grown up with, played with, greeted every day, they broke in and took everything! Everything! As if it were rightfully theirs!

"The clincher was this. You know that for each apartment building there is a trustee who collects the monthly fees for trash and water and so on?

Well, this man knocked on the door to collect from my father. But the trustee was holding my grandmother's money pouch!"

"Her money pouch?"

"Yes! And he went on like nothing had happened! What could my father say?"

What *could* he say? What *did* he say? What would *I* have said? What *do* I say? Today? Here, now, with Miriám-néni?

"I'm sorry. I'm really sorry."

She laughed. "You didn't do it! I've moved on! Music! Piano! Theory! This is my life now."

The next student knocking on the door brought our time to a close, issuing Miriám-néni further into her life as a teacher. The music from all around brought me no peace as I walked down those steps, issuing me further into a new world.

a night in the orphan house

MY 11 YEAR OLD SON, DAVID, AND I ARRIVED IN TIME FOR DINNER. THIS CONSISTED OF ROMANIAN FOOD AT A TABLE SURROUNDED BY A SEA OF EYES CASTING SHADOWS OF DOUBT, MISTRUST AND QUESTIONS.

We were two outsiders in the midst of a dozen gypsy boys who had been welcomed into this home with walls made of mud – real cow-dung mud. "This building is very typical of villages in the area," explained the orphanage director. "True, they don't last forever nor do they keep a family very warm in the winter. But it's what they have. It's what *we* have." We listened to the director who chose to live among the poorest of the poor after holding the managing partner's position of a large attorney's office in England.

The noise, the language, the smells – all new to me, more so to my son. I came with the hope of being able to help out in the future. David would often play ice hockey in Romania but had never slept in the bed of an orphan.

"This is Gergő. This is Ionuts. Raffi. Daniel. Ioan. And little Csaba," introduced the host. We smiled and nodded, trying to repeat the names correctly. We were hit with the mixed smell of bodies perspiring, fried sausage and sauerkraut, along with a whiff of the bleach water they used to fight off the dust creeping in from the dirt road one meter outside the front door.

The TV went on, the boys talked loudly using only a few syllables at a time, and we stuck close to our host. We found out that these were boys abandoned by either their mothers or fathers or grandparents or other relatives or gang leaders or state homes or all of the above. My son was meeting boys his age who had just months or weeks or days before adopted the train station as home base – living in and out of stationed cargo trains, in and out of Coke machines with their warm motors keeping refreshments cold, and cuddling up to the life-sustaining underground pipes that transferred hot water to nearby homes and factories.

I excused myself to use the bathroom where I washed my hands twice and then opened the door with my elbow. Coming out with a smile, I tried to summon up the love I had in me – somewhere – to embrace outcasts.

David was warned that at night one or more of the boys may wake up with loud shouts or even screams after reliving a nightmare. Memories of being discarded like trash kept coming back to the boys at night. Before coming to this house, they numbed these pains with constant glue sniffing, stealing and turf fighting.

"OK," was my son's response, not seeming to be too worried about it.

I tucked David in, shut off the lights and ducked over to the next bed with the ceiling closing in on my face. The noises still foreign, my thoughts continued to race like a non-stop merry-go-round. Landing nowhere but going round and around and around.

Morning seemed like a distant land down a long, dark tunnel. I finally heard the crowing of roosters announcing morning – well, the *coming* of morning. Night noises still hadn't quit: those of deep breathing, slight rustling, the occasional outburst and my own bed creaking with restlessness.

Finally, the sounds changed and the freedom to get out and get dressed released me from the so-called comfort of bed. Coffee, eggs, bread – filled a hunger within us.

With sleep still in his eyes, David soon joined us around the table. He seemed to blend into the sounds and movements of a new morning.

"Did you sleep OK, David?" the director asked.

"Yep," was all he got in return.

"Did you hear some strange noises in the night?"

"Once." And that was it. That was the extent of his discomfort.

Our van parked out front seemed like an old friend from another world. When we climbed in after saying our "good-byes," I felt at home once again, back to the safe and familiar. I could now take the wheel and steer the two and a half thousand pounds to where I wanted it to go. I understood the rules of the road, the duty of keeping alert and the quiet hum of that 2.4 liter diesel engine...running, pumping, turning all wheels and gears and systems to the ultimate goal...home.

"Are you glad we came, David?" I dared to ask.

"Yeah."

I let a time of silence go by before I dared to ask my real question. "Why?"

"Well, these are guys just like me...but without a dad. They need someone like you." I waited. Maybe he had another thought.

"Thanks for being my dad."

That was it. That was enough.

Coleman family prayer card (2006)

the missing flag

"SO, WHERE IS THE ROMANIAN FLAG?"

THE REFORMED PASTOR TURNED DIRECTLY AT ME, EYES BORING DEEP INTO MY SPIRIT AND WAY BEYOND THE SURFACE WORDS OF MY QUESTION. I REALIZED I HAD JUST HIT A HOT BUTTON...TO SAY THE LEAST. OH NO, WHAT'S COMING NEXT!? FOR THE REST OF MY LIFE, I WILL REFLECT ON THIS PASTOR'S ANSWER.

"I will NEVER, EVER have a Romanian flag here in my church!"

"We are in Romania!" I thought to myself. "What is he talking about?!"

"This is the 'Mother Land' for all of Hungary! Always was. Always will be! We are Hungarian and this is Hungary!" He looked away. End of message.

Well, not really. Although my question about the flag occurred years ago, I just recently got on the bus in Budapest with drunks singing about the Hungarian land lost to Romania, "Brothers in the 'Mother Land,' they took your land from you..." It's still a message being sung. But not heard.

I had taken the overnight train from Budapest to the eastern mountains of Romania. My son had a big ice hockey tournament there. When I woke up, I woke up to the most beautiful snow covered mountains. I was welcomed by people who travel by horse, bike, train, bus and a few by car. My foggy head from an all-night trip to remoteness gave way to the absolute warm hospitality of these people.

I remember seeing a strange map on the wall of a business within my first month living in Hungary. The map was labeled "Hungary." But its shape was so odd and much bigger than the Hungary I knew. I asked my neighbor about it. He just laughed a nervous laugh and said, "It's a long story." Then quietly, "Be careful who you talk with about this."

My daughter, Kristin, casually mentioned to one of my friends in Budapest that she had written a school paper on the Trianon Treaty (Treaty of Versailles) that took place after World War 1. He turned red in the face and said, "Wow! She wrote that? In school? Brave! Very brave!"

Over half a century later and this topic still boils under the surface for most Hungarians. I guess that being Hungarian is now more a matter of definition than of political borders. My Reformed pastor friend in Romania will never budge from his identity as a Hungarian.

"See, in this book!" he showed me back at his home. "Following 'The Treaty' in 1920, they purposefully imported Romanians into positions of power – government offices, legal representatives, police. And now our Hungarian children are *required* to study in the Romanian language!" The passion burst through, the veins in his neck popping out and my catching a few sprays from his lecture.

"Of course we protest. But what more can we do? This is our land! Has been since before the year 996 AD – before Budapest was ever established!"

I tried to comprehend his perspective, his world view, his land and people. I thought my previous question had to do with a flag but it really had to do with history and conquest and politics. This is why I see bumper stickers with that odd, old map of Hungary on cars in Budapest today.

After one meeting on June 4, 1920, two-thirds of Hungary became soil for Romania, Slovakia, Croatia, Austria, Slovenia, Ukraine and Yugoslavia. All in one day. In one signing. "It would be like having everything west of the Mississippi River taken away by Mexico and Canada," my daughter told me.

Who decided this and why? I was just asking a simple question of my pastor friend, "OK, here is the Hungary flag, the city flag and the Christian flag. But where is the Romanian flag?"

Before the final hockey game began we sang the traditional Hungarian "Mother Land" anthem. It brought tears to some of those who travelled with me from Budapest. I didn't ask anyone why we didn't sing the Romanian national anthem.

Coleman family prayer card (2011)

the mester

"Mester, I'm sorry to hear about your father." Silence.

Finally, "Do you want a beer?"

Soon, three of us were walking to the corner for a drink. The Mester invited another to join us, now crowding out any deep discussion about the death of his father. I had made time to offer my condolences to my son's old coach who had become one of my first friends in this foreign land of Hungary. But while sipping on my soda I didn't hear about the recent tragedy. Instead, I heard about the weather and the past ice hockey season in Győr where we used to live and where my son learned to play.

"Dévid! Push it! Pass it! Shoot it! Skate! Hit! Faster!" The Mester, also known as Gábor bácsi, would cry out. He was called "Mester" (MESH-ter) because he knew the game so well. A twelve-year professional ice hockey player, now full-time coach, this man in his mid-forties was respected in several countries in Europe for his domination on the ice.

But today, I was hoping to get to something deeper, inaccessible, something like gold hidden deep below the earth's surface. Coaches in Hungary never talk about personal feelings, hurts, angers, disappointments. It just comes out in different forms. This man in front of me learned to take it out on the ice. He fought. The rage would erupt. When feelings began to surface he would drop his gloves and dish out severe blows to the other guy's face. Today, the gloves gave way to a couple of beers and shallow talk. But I knew he was hurting.

We finally finished our drinks and began to walk back to the ice rink. The Mester and I sat outside in the sun, in front of the lifeless, empty ice rink. Warm weather, no ice. This was always the curse of an ice hockey club playing on an outdoor sheet of ice. Sun. Heat. Spring. Only a dog barked next door. My scheduled time for this visit had already passed.

"Yeah, my brother found him in the middle of the night. He had shaved, gotten dressed in his best, climbed up to the top storage space of the barn and kicked a box out from under his feet."

Quiet. It begins to sink in. The nightmare begins to be relived.

"He had NEVER been to the hospital in his life until just before Easter. They found he had colon cancer and he needed radiation treatment. After the second week of treatment, he came home from the Romanian hospital and we were all shocked to see him not even dress for the special Easter services! Every Sunday of his life, he dressed up and went to Mass. This Sunday – Easter of all Sundays! – he didn't even shave, didn't even go out of the house." The Mester shakes his head in disbelief.

"He didn't want to be a burden on anyone. He felt he'd be a burden to my mom, to me, to the whole family. So, he made a choice….

"Yeah, I talked to him on Easter Sunday….But then on Easter Monday, my brother called me in the middle of the night…."

Silence. The same dog barks next door. The concrete rink reflects the grief, the silence, the life gone out of the game. There's hardly any interest in an ice rink without ice. But something deeper is going on here. The story of death and loss emerges. I wait for it – now in my third hour of looking for that small opening into the deep mine of hurt feelings.

"Jerry, is there any hope for him? You know, the priest didn't even have his robe on for the funeral. There was no singing. And he was buried in the far corner of the cemetery where all the disgraced are buried."

I try to comprehend this. A life of honor for 76 years turns to a burial of shame in one day. And shame cannot be buried in the same way or in the same space.

I finally try to address this eternal issue. "Well, I'm glad I'm not the judge. And no priest is the judge, either. God alone is the judge. He knows your father."

"He was a good man. He went to Mass every single Sunday. Sat in the same seat. Except this last one. Will he make it?"

Silence. What do I say? What *can* I say?

"All I know is that we can personally know Jesus and trust in Him. He makes the way to our Father in Heaven. It's not all about what we do on certain days. It's about believing in Jesus."

"Well, he was a good man. He knew Jesus if anyone did."

The Mester's father – once a patriarch in his village in the mountains of East Romania; respected by all within the five mile radius in which he lived his whole life; pillar and steward of the local church; and father of my son's first ice hockey coach – now shamed in death and buried in the far corner of the village cemetery.

But now, only memories remain. My memories of life with ice; his memories of a respected father. Our now shared memory about the mystery of life, death and eternity. I know he carries a share of my first days and years of confusion in a foreign land. He knows I now carry a share of his first days of confusion about a foreign Heaven.

a missionary life is a lonely life

A missionary life is a lonely life...

A life alone, a lone life
Setting out from home

Arriving, striving, unpacking
Wondering, shaking, finding no rest

Walking, wondering, wandering
Waking, wanting, waning

A missionary life is a homeless life...

Having left home
To make a home
Away from home

The people I have never known
The people now in my home
The people I must go and see

...surrounded by people!

Landing among a mass
Of families and clans.

In the middle of precious souls
Calling silently for help.

In one culture after another
Of the highest created order.

...being at home wherever we go!

Adjusting and knowing
One culture, then another
While embracing people.

And welcome
And love
And grace.

A missionary life is a poor life...

Without security
Asset broke
Few things
Not holding on

Asking for gifts
And money
And help
And asking for more

Lonely.
Homeless.
Poor.

...filled with boundless riches!

Yet being given
More and more
Of the stuff
Money cannot buy.

Receiving a bounty
Of riches
Of grace
Of life.

Surrounded.
Being at home.
Filled with boundless riches.

harmonizing home

a growing chorus in europe

"They held harps given them by God and sang the song of Moses the servant of God and the song of the Lamb: 'Great and marvelous are your deeds, Lord God Almighty. Just and true are your ways, King of the ages. Who will not fear you, O Lord, and bring glory to your name? For you alone are holy. All nations will come and worship before you, for your righteous acts have been revealed.'" – Revelation 15:2c-4

I CAN PICTURE A HUGE CHORUS OF PEOPLE SINGING THESE SONGS TO THE LORD GOD ALMIGHTY IN ALL 269 INDIGENOUS LANGUAGES OF EUROPE! CAN YOU?

In fact, I pray this. I expect this. I give my life to hear the chorus! OK, I'm not giving voice lessons, but I'm traveling, preaching and praying for the nations of Europe to *sing the song* of Jesus!

The need here is huge. I see such spiritual decay. I feel at times like I'm walking around in a cemetery or at least in a museum lacking spiritual life. Europe is now secular where it once was the wonderful foundation of faith in Christ alone! Many cathedrals stand empty, except for camera-carrying tourists from all over the world who are not singing songs, just snapping photos.

"I'm a Christian! I was baptized at birth!" I hear so often. But I'm still looking for the evidence of the Lordship of Jesus Christ and the song of Christ expressed in the daily lives of Europeans.

Sheet music isn't music till it's sung. Baptism isn't Christian till it's personally harmonized with Jesus.

The Church, which was birthed in Europe, took center stage, and literally became the geographical center of village and city life, now seems marginalized. The mention of God is excluded in the new European Community Constitution.

But we know there is hope. Jesus tells story after story of coming back home, of being invited to the banquet, of the prodigal son returning to his loving Father.

A remnant remains. New hope breaks out! There are people scattered over Europe who have kept the faith and lift up new songs in the name of Jesus.

Not long ago, four of us crammed into the small, rented space two of us used as an office. One posed this question to me, "What's the fastest way to transform society?"

I thought to myself, "We need a miracle! Lots of big ones!" Instead, I said, "OK, I give up."

the doubling effect

TO REACH ALL IN THE WORLD ONE-BY-ONE.

IF ONE PERSON WOULD REACH ONE PERSON AND CONTINUE TO REACH ONE PERSON … 34 TIMES!

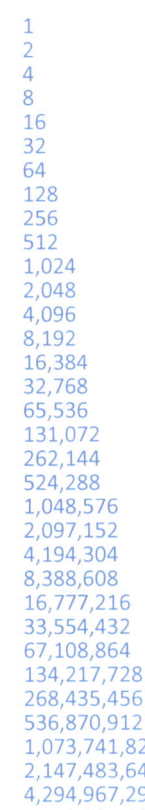

1
2
4
8
16
32
64
128
256
512
1,024
2,048
4,096
8,192
16,384
32,768
65,536
131,072
262,144
524,288
1,048,576
2,097,152
4,194,304
8,388,608
16,777,216
33,554,432
67,108,864
134,217,728
268,435,456
536,870,912
1,073,741,824
2,147,483,648
4,294,967,296
8,589,934,592

58   harmonizing home | one-way ticket

He answered, "One person at a time."

Oh, I can do that! I can touch one. I can witness to one. I can bring Jesus to my neighbor! I can suggest, "Let's sing a duet to the Lord!" Because a few duets gathered together make a nice chorus. And a few chorus groups gathered in the name of Jesus make a grand choir. And a few choirs gathered together, well, that's the singing we hear in Revelation!

tears flowed

Lanzarote, Canary Islands, Spain
January 21

TEARS FLOWED AROUND THE QUIET ROOM. IT HAPPENED. IT'S COMPLETED. A QUIET HOLY REVERENCE HOVERED FOR A FEW MINUTES THAT SEEMED TO SPAN THE FIVE YEARS THAT LED TO THIS MOMENT.

Stories told, songs sung, sermon preached, documents signed, handshakes and hugs given. The Emanuel Church was now part of the Free Methodist Church. The Free Methodist Church was now part of the Emanuel Church. This bond strengthens all. As we joined together at this moment, the reality of it all began to settle in.

Just before the quiet hush, I was trying to figure out how I got here on this remote island. OK, in Spain, but really just 60 kilometers off the coast of Africa. I landed on an island of 100,000 people where 5 million people fly through the local airport each year. I was rubbing shoulders with people who have lived their lives literally surrounded by the Atlantic Ocean.

I became part of a historical moment that involved a remote American leaving home in Budapest early on Friday morning, running (literally) through two airports – one in Milan and the other in Barcelona – to get on a third plane for a two and a half hour flight in a large jet from the mainland of Spain.

Music, outreach, food, flyers, documents, extra chairs, invitations and logistics had recently dominated the attention of most of the 70 people gathered in this worship center. There had been a flurry of activity as all the arrangements and final touches fell into place.

Pastor Vito leaned over to me and whispered, "Years ago I could never picture this freedom and growth! We were trapped in a strict and controlling church environment. But now…" His smile was HUGE! His eyes released tears that ran untouched down his cheeks.

"Now, I feel such a freedom and love…yet a protection. We're now part of a larger family which loves us, encourages us and keeps us accountable. And the new people keep coming – young people, children, adults."

Words being inadequate, I returned to that quiet reverence knowing that something here went way beyond what I could see with physical eyes. Hurry gave way to hush. No one moved. Yes, that's it!

The Spirit of God filled that place! The Spirit of confirmation came down upon us all. God touched us. Moved us. To soft, flowing tears.

it's a long way to tipperary

"It's a long way to Tipperary! It's a long way to go!" We were singing a few lines on the bus. Twenty of us. From Dublin to Tipperary in Ireland for the European Methodist Council.

Our Irish pastor friend serving in Hungary told me that I was going to the town about which this song was written. I had learned it in elementary school. A World War I song. I remember these old war songs we sang with energy and light-heartedness.

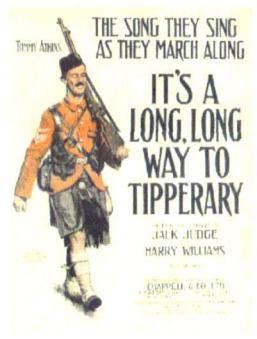

The war had been so far away and so long ago. But it struck me that, "Wow! I'm actually going to Tipperary!"

The Allies sang about this. Our forces must have been in the middle of battle and longed to go back home – to places like Tipperary.

It was fun to sing the song once again but now singing in a chorus of mixed cultures. In Ireland! "I think I am the only American on this bus," I quietly realized.

Then I froze!
    My heart stopped.
        My mind stopped.
            My mouth couldn't move.
                It felt suddenly dry.

I was sitting between two Germans! Germans! The enemy! OK, the former enemy, trying to convince myself. But aren't these the people we hated, we fought, we wanted to annihilate?

Germans. The Central Powers. On the bus. Singing a war song I learned 40 years ago. I'm in the middle of – what? War? Confusion? Conflict?

No – Peace!

These two Germans are the most loving and kind people I have met on this trip. Look at their faces. Two Methodist pastors. They seek the same as I do – to share the peace and joy of Jesus Christ in all Europe.

My heart settled down. My voice picked up. My mind tried to reconcile this setting, this miracle, this sudden joining of forces.

"It's a long way to Tipperary! It's a long way to go." I kept singing quietly to myself. We arrived. We all ate a meal and shared Holy Communion together. It was a long way. But together we gathered around the unifying table of Christ.

flight to lisbon

Flights: Budapest – Milan; Milan – Lisbon
Date: November 24

04:15
My alarm goes off. I jump out of bed and carry my bags down the four flights of steps to the street.

05:01
The airport minibus is right on time.

06:00
I check in at the *Alitalia* counter, move through passport control and security. Then get a cup of coffee.

> Over coffee, I journal and pray. Where is God taking me? In the midst of such flurry and activity, the question enters my 50 year old brain. Am I still on the path of God? Or am I just running circles? Will He continue to lead me according to His will? Or am I going to miss it?

08:50
We land in Milan right on time. But now the long taxi to the terminal... but there's no gate. We have to walk down the portable steps onto the tarmac to ride a bus. I had almost booked a different flight because the 60 minutes in Milan is hardly enough time to take bus rides, get through security – AGAIN – and through passport control – AGAIN – and then on to my departing gate.

09:05
My next flight is at 09:50. Boarding at 09:20. But we're still trying to get off this plane and crowd on this bus! But we're weaving all over the airport. I'm first off the bus! Good planning to get a spot by the door on the right side of the bus. I'm proud of myself. But people are running past me.

09:15
A long line of people to get through security. OK. A quick scan tells me there are five lines. I jump over to what looks like the shortest. Waiting. Waiting.

09:18
My next flight boards in two minutes! Italian officials! I think this gal is more interested in the social activity here than getting us processed as quickly as possible!! Why is she chuckling with her colleagues and chatting with the passengers?! She finally waves me through the metal detector, greets me with a smile and checks my boarding pass. Italians. I LOVE them. But NOT as security officials when I have a plane to catch!

09:21
Got through. Up the stairs. There's a monitor! Where's my gate? A-21. OK. Here we go. I'm NOT going to run all the way through this airport. But I am going to walk quickly. Very quickly.

"Pardon." "Pardon." Why do people stand on the left on these walkways?! A-21. I've been this way before. Yes. I know where I'm going now.

> I'm thankful for these midpoint checks in life. God confirms His call, His vision, His direction once in a while. Yes, I know I'm where I need to be in life. It's just a difficult moment. It's just hard to see right now. There are some things I just can't control or determine. There are some issues I can't seem to get through. But I'm keeping you, dear Jesus, in the forefront of my thoughts and prayers.

09:26!
I made it to the gate and there's still a line! I'm not the last. Now, back on another bus. And this one is absolutely packed. Uh. We wait for 15 minutes. Sweat drips down my back. I had plenty of time! The bus doors

finally close and we're off through the airport maze.

I'm in no rush to get off the bus and climb up the steps to my plane. But when I do, I'm greeted with, "Buon Giorno!"

Hey! Isn't this the flight attendant who greeted me in Budapest!? I find my seat. There's another flight attendant I recognize!

"Excuse me," I ask. "Did you just come from Budapest?"

"Yes, we did."

"So, I was on this plane!?"

"Yes, you were."

He just smiles, shrugs his shoulders and moves on.

I sit here. A 60 minute mini-marathon took me right back to within seven rows of my first seat. A new sense of perspective begins to sink in.

> The Kingdom of Heaven has different space and time. It's not all about what I can see with my eyes and count on my clock. The Kingdom of Heaven is not all about my rush from one flight to another. But it's about my moving in the spiritual realm and trusting the activity of the Holy Spirit. Yes, I want to reset my vision and my clock to this reality. Maybe if I would just sit and wait on God, I would be further ahead.
>
> "Lord, it's true. I can't see the big picture. But I trust You with it. I rest in You.
>
> "Forgive me for my selfish ambition and private positioning. Forgive me for running a circle on my own strength when You have so much more for me.
>
> "And all I have to do is sit still and wait.
>
> "Then fly with You."

you MUST give more!

"YOU MUST GIVE MORE" IS FICTITIOUS BUT BASED ON STORIES I HAVE HEARD FROM EUROPEANS OVER THE YEARS. I PUT MYSELF IN THE SHOES OF THE MAN WHO STRUGGLED TO FIND BALANCE BETWEEN HIS FAMILY'S NEEDS AND HIS RELIGIOUS "RIGHT DOINGS." THE STORY IS SET A COUPLE OF GENERATIONS AGO BUT SOME OF THE EFFECTS OF THESE REALITIES STILL EXIST TODAY.

"YOU MUST GIVE MORE! IT IS YOUR DUTY AS A CITIZEN OF THIS VILLAGE! AND THIS COUNTRY! AND OF THE HIGH KINGDOM OF GOD! IF YOU DON'T GIVE YOUR FULL CHURCH ALLOCATION, THEN YOU WILL NOT BE BURIED IN THE VILLAGE CEMETERY!"

I looked at the priest's collector in disbelief. Just trying to put bread on the table for my children and dying mother and last of all for myself, I felt like the Israelites when demanded of them to make bricks without straw.

"How can I give what I do not have? How will I feed my family?"

"We know that you want to be protected in this life and the life hereafter by our Savior and His appointed clergy of His Church. Do you really wish to play around with the Holy Father and your eternal destiny?"

How is this? I'm so confused. I hear through the Lectionary readings that Jesus is the Way, that He is the Shepherd – the Good Shepherd who lays down His life for the sheep. Yet here in front of me stands this human being, yes, sent from the priest and representing The Church, but holding my eternal future in the one line of his ledger. Why so complicated? Why so forceful? Is God a God of starvation and punishment? Or is He really the peaceful, loving Father that I sometimes imagine?

"OK, just one moment please." I turned, walking blindly past my family's eyes all paired up to ask the obvious question, "What are we going to do?!" I continued, ignoring the inner noise of my doubts and fears, to the side of my bed, and lifted the mattress revealing my secret stash to all the hungry eyes.

The questions just have to stop. So my silly doubts gave way to a desperate hope for security. My begrudged gift brought a smile to the intermediary from Heaven still waiting impatiently outside my open door. His hands wrote my update in his life-giving ledger which didn't really bring a smile to my face, but gave a degree of relief to my torn soul. Secure… for now. I did my part.

My dream of a new horse now traded in for the dream of eternal security. My inherited blessing from my earthly father now exchanged for a blessing from the one who represents the Heavenly Father.

The collector quickly mumbled a comment about the ledger, recited the memorized blessing for this moment and left the final remembrance of the village religious stronghold, "See you on Sunday, then."

"See you on Sunday."

a spontaneous dance broke out!

A SPONTANEOUS DANCE BROKE OUT! I COULD NEVER HAVE PREDICTED IT WOULD HAPPEN HERE OF ALL PLACES. BURIED IN THE MIDDLE OF UKRAINE, DOWN A LONG, DARK, PITTED ROAD MILES AWAY FROM ANYTHING FAMILIAR, WE SPILLED OUT OF A VAN AND MADE OUR WAY TOWARD THE ORPHANAGE FOR ABANDONED CHILDREN. EVEN THOUGH SMILES GREETED ME AS I FIRST WALKED INTO THIS HOME FOR THE UNWANTED, I KNEW THAT JUST BELOW THE PAINTED SMILES WERE STORIES OF BEATING, SICKNESS, ESCAPE AND SURVIVAL. WE ENTERED A GATHERING OF THE DISCARDED.

Yet, something happened that night which can't be given justice with my words. The spur-of-the-moment musical party that burst on the scene will forever be embedded in the Memorex of my mind. Time, space, setting, culture, background all took a back seat to the immediate songs of Heaven.

"Of course, bring along your violin!" I responded to Mansell Morgan. Pastor of a Free Methodist Church in Manchester, England, and former performer in the BBC Philharmonic, he was leading a team of people reaching out to the poor in Ukraine. I joined a few of their visits. But this one particular visit will forever be remembered as I witnessed an unusual union of spirit.

Following the customary charming performances from the children, Mansell Morgan pulled out his violin and proceeded to shock me. He let the orphan kids touch it! Touch it!? His German violin and French bow were worth over $6,000!! Mansell just smiled, assuring me that each one of these kids was worth so much more.

The Orphanage Director pulled me over and told me through a translator that the retired, widowed teacher sitting "right there" plays the accordion. "Oh, that's nice," I replied, keeping polite conversation going. "Has she played for long?" After the Orphanage Director ordered a few Ukrainian commands, the retired teacher reluctantly disappeared and emerged bashfully carrying her well worn instrument.

And slowly the magical moment unfolded. One chord. Two chords. And a song filled the air on the accordion. Ah. This sound so full! Her touch was amazing! I didn't know the tune, but the melody soared. Mansell's violin found its way back into his hands. Two strokes, and he was right with her. Wait! How did he know that tune!?

All the small talk stopped. Everyone in the room was drawn in. We began to realize that some unseen Conductor with an unseen score had brought together the most wonderful concert ever heard. Words were kept hidden away as not to spoil the moment – or even try to explain it. Occasional glances around the room assured the unspoken acknowledgment that something very special was happening.

Melody. Harmony. One led. The other followed. One tune. Russian. Another tune. British. German. Ah. A famous piece – Beethoven. A folk tune. A dance. Energy filled the room as we witnessed the connection of two masters from estranged and distant cultures. Sounds of Heaven. Music across the ages. Notes of praise. Harmonies and melodies of the heart.

While some sat with mouths slightly opened, two women broke out in dance. Another looked for a partner for some kind of movement that would coincide with the melodies saturating the room.

The smiles in the room grew deeper. There, at that moment, God touched hearts among the unwanted and discarded. Heaven came to earth and we heard the sounds of the angels' chorus. One moment changed a bit of history, spanned cultures and moved our spirits. Smiles slowly transformed from the surface of each face into the depths of each spirit. Yes, our spirits danced that night.

a walk around the walls of jerusalem

I WALKED ON TOP OF THE WALLS THAT COULDN'T SPEAK. YES, I WALKED AROUND THE ANCIENT CITY OF JERUSALEM. ON TOP OF THE WALLS. THAT TODAY ARE MUTE. BUT SPEAK VOLUMES.

My wife, Jan, and I landed in Tel Aviv without a ride and without a place to stay. We trusted something would open up. And something did – but not how we expected.

We ended up in the car of a Jewish man whose daughter we met back in the New York City airport. The whole line of people saw the CNN breaking news on the nearby TV screen. We saved her place in line so she could phone home to Jerusalem to hear if one of those just killed in a car bomb was one of her friends. CNN broadcasted from her neighborhood. Which of her neighbors had died?

I thought of that bomb while walking around the walls of Jerusalem. I thought of the ancient wars in the Holy Land while hearing the description of this city by our guide with a big hat. While my consuming wonder sent me back in history, the young woman's CNN breaking news had triggered a horrendous night on the plane from New York City to Tel Aviv…wondering…wondering if one of her closest friends had been lost. In New York City she couldn't get through to anyone.

"This is the East Gate," our tour guide began. This East Gate had first opened the way for us into this new experience of ancient Jerusalem. My walk in Jerusalem dream coming true – but not as expected.

"Up this way is Herod's Gate. This is where all the animals would be issued in for sacrifice at the Holy Temple." I could picture it, almost smell it. The Temple used to sit on the Temple Mount – right over there. Yes, ever since I was old enough to look at pictures, I remember seeing the drawings of The Holy Temple on The Temple Mount. But now, I'm here, in Jerusalem, overlooking a golden Muslim Mosque.

Things have changed. We're told that the ancient city of Jerusalem actually stood right here, but quite a few meters lower than the present. Building, destruction and rebuilding over centuries raised the height of the city. And the height of distress.

When we landed in Tel Aviv, I saw this young woman run into the arms of her father and seconds later begin sobbing. Was this in grief or relief?

We stood at a distance but finally heard, "Dad, this is the couple who befriended me in the New York airport."

"Hi, I'm Jerry and this is Jan. We're glad to meet you."

"I'm Joshua. Thank you so much for helping Greta in New York. Where are you staying? Do you have a ride to Jerusalem?" he asked.

"No, we don't have a ride into Jerusalem and we don't know where we are staying," I responded, which sparked a curious wonder on his face, followed by a bit of an adventurous smile.

"We can give you a ride. Come on!"

While in the car, Greta told us in great relief that her father reported none of her friends had been killed in the bomb. Joshua went on to describe some of the ugly fighting going on, yet how he is involved in leading peace talks with Jews, Muslims and Christians.

Welcomed into their home, Joshua immediately began working through the phone book. "Well, no room there. I'll try the Episcopal Guesthouse. It's run by Christian Palestinians. I know it well."

He ended up driving us into that "enemy territory" to the place we would call home for awhile. All arranged, we gave our heart-felt thanks and deep appreciation.

We woke up and began the walk around the walls of the ancient city with wonder, with awe, with fear, with disappointment. The East Gate. Herod's Gate. Then a man in our group, a Christian from America, began speaking loudly to our guide. I guess this American disagreed on our Jewish guide's take on the ancient. "That is NOT TRUE!" he argued. "I've had enough!" He suddenly left the guide with a $20 bill and disappeared.

Enough? I wonder if our Father in Heaven has had enough. These walls are not so ancient for Him. These stories are not so old. These wars and rumors of wars, the tearing down and building up are all too common.

The walls themselves stood and fell against one battered time after another. Ancient and current stories clashed within the same geography. My childhood pictures became distorted as I walked on the wall and listened to the stories.

But one reality stands firm. One message clear. Jesus. He tore down the barriers and dividing walls for the sake of a new city, a new Jerusalem... where all will live in everlasting peace.

I long to walk the walls of His city.

being home

| father's day |

HE QUIETNESS RINGS HOME THE TRUTHS OF THE DAY
LIKE THE LONG, LINGERING TONE AT THE TOP OF EACH HOUR.

It's here.
        It's now.
                It's true.
                        Father.
                                Father.
                                        Father.

Now, which part of being a father do I see?
I see no children at the moment.
I hear no voices at the moment.
But I see the lingering truths of my three living beings
who carry much of who I am.

Life came from me to them.

Breath flowed through the lungs that I watched develop and mature.
Speech followed my patterns.
Sights were daily shared.
Life experiences blended together into a stew fit for a king.

Sarah
finally arrived in the heat of the summer
forever changing the way we think of family.
Two became three.
The third dominated thought patterns and life plans.
Huge adaptations for another living being.
And the long awaited rose began to blossom
right before my teary eyes.

Kristin
flowed into life patterns of the three.
This fourth added dimensions so complex and so rich
that exponentially expanded the meaning of community.
The home became a playground of all dimensions
like a year-round water park filled with slides, tubes, rivers,
shoots and surprise splashes of laughter.

David
completed the score with unending motion.
A family of five made for a family alive.
Unto us a son was born.
He was called David.
He wears the mantle of manhood
joining the battle for the heart of his other half.

Because Fatherhood
never begins without the soil, the home, the fertility of the other.
My image cannot be seen without the reflection of another.

Jan
is the bearer of life on life.
She is the earth of our community.
Each of us breathes the breaths of hope
from the womb of the woman.
It is the loving heart of one so receptive that
brings meaning to the one called father.

So, who am I?
What part had I?
I wonder as the ring begins to fade.
The quiet is much quieter now.
The noise is taken to other places and faces
and communities much further and farther.
I?

I reflect the heart of a father,
no, The Father.

He is the giver of life and life and life and love.
The Father in Heaven began with a breath.
The breath of love fulfilled
the longing for family, for hope, for faith and belief.

Yes, The Father shows me
the way to create and embrace.
And to multiply and release.
He helps me see and hear
the bell from the tower of truth, ringing freedom.
Yes, from there the truth sets each one free.
Free to be.

For I am father.
This is *our* day.

my home base

FINALLY! AFTER YEARS AWAY, I WAS GREETED BACK AT THE ANNUAL CONFERENCE WHERE MY PASTOR FRIENDS GATHER YEAR AFTER YEAR. MY HOME BASE. AFTER DREAMING ABOUT BEING IN AND AMONG MY FRIENDS AND CO-WORKERS FOR SO LONG, THERE I WAS! HOME! AMONG. MY FRIENDS AND ENCOURAGERS. BUT SOMETHING HAD CHANGED. SOMETHING OUT OF PLACE.

It was at this meeting years ago that a crowd of people gathered around us and prayed for the five of us. We were blessed as a family to sell our house, leave our home and represent those who want to share the love of Jesus around the world. It was out of the richness of their prayer, vision and support that we set out with a one-way ticket.

Pastors Kenny, Mark, Peter, Bobby, Travis, Gerry and I had trusted each other enough to agree on agendas of confession, truth telling, encouragement and prayer. I came to anticipate meeting with the district pastors twice a month. One of us would be on the "hot seat" each meeting, drilled with any conceivable question by the others. "I'm on the hot seat today!" What would they ask me? What would I tell them? After awhile, I realized it didn't matter. We really grew to trust and love one another. I missed them so much over the years!

On a hot Friday afternoon, I walked back into the Conference setting. But little remained as I remembered. It had moved from the historic college campus setting. I now sat at a round table instead of on the familiar padded pew. I attended a "Leadership Summit" and not "Annual Conference." I just tried to blend back in and among that which had been home for me. But still, something wasn't right.

Some shouted across the room and embraced me right away. To others, I introduced myself. Several of my pastor friends had moved to another conference or had even quit the ministry. Some worship songs I knew. Others brand new to me. Is this where I belong?

All those years ago, we began to make new friends in a new culture...far, far away from my district friends. We began with one person while praying for God to raise up new leaders across the continent. I dreamed about starting a new Annual Conference in Europe. I felt in the "hot seat" every day, trying to address the complexity of questions and issues of our planting churches in Europe, the continent with such rich Christian heritage.

> ### acts 13:2-3
>
> While they were worshiping the Lord and fasting, the Holy Spirit said, "Set apart for me Barnabas and Saul for the work to which I have called them." So after they had fasted and prayed, they placed their hands on them and sent them off.

Zoltán, Károly, Simon, Ákos, Misi, Gergély and Márton. These men of new faith had been putting me on the hot seat. Post-communist life, broken relationships, a struggling economy and being taught "there is no living God" trigger questions difficult to answer. What can I say? How will I say it in these new languages? I now realize that the universal language of love cuts through barriers and questions and doubts. This is why I moved here. I am here for them and they are here for me.

So, back at that once familiar Annual Conference Leadership Summit, I was surrounded by the new and the old. I was welcomed back. I was prayed for once again. But all had changed. Most of all, *I* had changed.

Where is my place? Where do I belong? Where is my home base?

A few days following Leadership Summit, I boarded the plane back to Europe, back to the people whose names I couldn't even pronounce a few years ago. Same flight pattern as our first one-way ticket: Detroit, Amsterdam, Budapest.

But the plane took me to an ancient land with emerging young leaders in faith. I'm back home.

oh pain, pain

August 20 – 5:20 pm

This poem was written just before our last family meal before moving out of our rented apartment. Jan and I had spent a year in the USA. Kristin had moved back home for that year. David was moving out for college. The next day we would officially be "Empty Nest."

Oh pain, pain.
    The earth moving,
        the children leaving,
            the bags packing
                and my head is swirling.
Oh pain, pain.
    The stress building,
        the answers eluding,
            the questions mounting
                and my mind is twirling.
Oh pain, pain.
    The past dizzy,
        the future fuzzy,
            the moment hazy
                and my memory is fading.
Oh joy, joy.
    The food preparing,
        the drinks pouring,
            the table setting
                and my family sits around…
One last time.

| miles and miles

2,000 MILES. FROM THE SAFE, SECURE WOMB OF SMALL TOWN ILLINOIS TO THE EXPANSIVE, VOLATILE METROPOLIS OF LA (HOLLYWOOD, TO BE EXACT). I SHARE THE DRIVING OF THE ONE-WAY MOVING TRUCK WITH MY DAUGHTER WHO CAN BARELY SEE OVER THE STEERING WHEEL. DO I SHARE HER ANTICIPATION OF A NEW, BETTER LIFE IN THAT DISTANT LAND SO FAR FROM HOME?

Illinois, Missouri, Oklahoma. Just 334 more miles of New Mexico. Then Arizona. Finally California. The air keeps getting hotter. The land grows barren. Water stops, fuel stops now scarce, but my eyes often fill up.

What will we do when we get there? Unload.

What will we do after we unload? Arrange the apartment.

What will we do next? The one-way rental gets turned in.

My round trip will continue by airplane 7,000 miles back to where I call home these days.

Her one-way trip ends here. In her own apartment. With the stuff we brought. In LA. Under the "HOLLYWOOD" sign.

The art of being a father never grows easy. One day she's born. The next she's in school. Soon after, she's gone to a land of strangers. Can she really call this – "home"?

The art of being a father means watching from an ever-increasing distance, like backing away from a mosaic hoping to see the big picture. I hope to see some of it. Small pieces fit together one to another and a setting emerges. A roommate. A neighborhood. Some new friends coming in to help. A place of worship. This could be someone's home … in time.

7,000 miles back home.
One seat.
Alone.
Time seems to stand still on this endless flight.

Two decades just flew past me.
I am a father to a child who now is there and not here.
My home is not her home.
Her home is not my home … anymore.

revelation 3:7-8

To the angel of the church in Philadelphia write:

These are the words of him who is holy and true, who holds the key of David. What he opens no one can shut, and what he shuts no one can open. I know your deeds. See, I have placed before you an open door that no one can shut. I know that you have little strength, yet you have kept my word and have not denied my name.

the kids are coming!

The kids are coming!
All are coming!
For the holidays and beyond!

                        Kids? Kids?
                        No, they are adults.
                        Grown up and beyond.

The kids are coming!
For Christmas, for weeks!
They come with gifts and news!

                        Kids? Children, yes.
                        But for a visit.
                        With a few gifts and some news.

The kids are coming!
Soon be here!
To play and eat and celebrate!

                        Kids? Grown adults, rather.
                        Coming from new homes.
                        To talk and cook and celebrate.

The kids are coming!
All will be well!
The family together forever!

                        Kids? Family, yes.
                        All is as it should be.
                        The family autonomous forever

            In new homes and beyond.

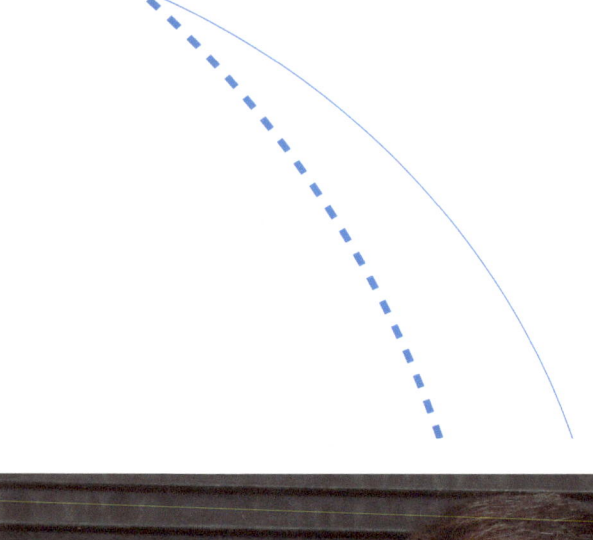

we are home

I left home
    Long ago
        From where I was born
           and nurtured.

We left home
    Years ago
        Where everything became
           distant memory.

We expanded home
    Year by year
        Until more people
           felt at home.

We felt at home
    Little by little
        As more homes were
           opened to us.

We harmonize home
    Day after day
        To those waiting for
           the heavenly song.

Home circles grow
    Person to person
    In one language
        after another.

Our three began leaving home
    Child after child
    Back to where
        they had been born.

We are home
    I, you, Jesus, we
    Wherever we are,
        we are home.

CPSIA information can be obtained
at www.ICGtesting.com
Printed in the USA
LVHW072030080120
642998LV00001B/1/P